The Book of Indian Sweets

GW01044857

SATARUPA BANERJEE

Rupa & Co

Contents

Rosogolla
(RASGULLA)

Rosogolla with its history of more than a century has crossed the boundaries of culture, caste and creed. It was invented in 1868 in a tiny sweetmeat shop at Baghbazar in North Calcutta.

Its creator, Nobin Chandra Das, was desperate to invent a new sweet that could compete with *sandesh*. He endeavoured to create a sweet that was soft and succulent as against the dry texture of *sandesh*. He did succeed, albeit after initial failures. It is interesting to note that *rosogolla* did not gain instant popularity. In fact, it took several years before it found favour with the Bengalis. Later, it was Nobin Chandra's son, better known as K.S. Das, who promoted its sale in India and abroad. Now, the tinned variety is available everywhere.

You need

Home made *paneer* made out of 1 lt of cow's milk; 750 ml water; 1¼ kg sugar; 1 tsp flour; 1 tbsp rose water.

NOW:

1. The *paneer* must be totally free of water. This is very important.
2. Put the *paneer*, one teaspoon of flour and one teaspoon of granulated sugar and knead with the palm of your hand against a wooden surface or a tray.

   The kneaded *paneer* should be absolutely smooth, but take care not to put too much pressure on it.
3. Make small marble-sized crack-free balls out of these. Remember, *rosogullas* swell at least four times their orginal size.
4. Now, make a thin syrup with the sugar and water.
5. Test the syrup between the forefinger and thumb. When slightly sticky, drop in the *rosogulla* balls, one by one carefully. Cover the vessel and boil for ten minutes.

Rosogolla

Rajbhog

6. In the meantime, the syrup will thicken somewhat. Put in two tablespoons of hot water slowly.

7. Reduce flame. Let the syrup simmer.

8. Add another two tablespoons of hot water. This will make the *rosogullas* soft and spongy.

9. Finally, the *rosogullas* will puff up and float to the top.

10. Take a large vessel, put two tablespoons of cold water and carefully put in the *rosogullas* and the syrup in it.

11. Refrigerate when cool.

12. Before serving, add rose water.

Rajbhog
(GIANT RASOGULLA)

These are giant *rosogullas*, only the texture differs a little.

You need
250 gm *paneer* made out of cow's milk; 1 tsp flour; 1 tsp semolina; 1 tsp rose water; 60 gm *khoya*; seeds of 1 black cardamom; 1 kg sugar; 750 ml water.

NOW:
1. Knead *paneer* with your hands well until smooth. Mix flour and semolina and knead well again.
2. Make 12 smooth crack-free balls. Mix *khoya* and black cardamom seeds. Divide this into 12 portions.
3. In the meantime, make a thin syrup with the sugar and water.

4. Stuff one portion of the *khoya* mixture in each *paneer* ball. Roll the balls in your palm so that they close properly. Otherwise, they may disintegrate in the syrup.

5. Boil the *paneer* balls in the syrup like *rosogullas* to puff them up to a bigger size. While boilding, sprinkle the syrup with 1 tablespoon of hot water.

6. Continue cooking the *rajbhog* on high heat till they begin to crack a little on the surface. (About 7–10 minutes).

7. Remove from fire. Sprinkle rose water.

8. Let them soak in the syrup for at least four hours before serving.

Variation:

If you want yellow-coloured *rajbhog,* knead half teaspoon of saffron with the *paneer.* Or, use *kesar* dissolved in rose water.

You may stuff *rajbhog* with pista instead of *khoya*.

Cham Cham
(FLATTENED PANEER SWEET IN SYRUP)

These can be coloured yellow, pink or left white.

You need
Paneer made out of 1 lt milk; 2 cups sugar; 7 cups of water, 1¼ tsp flour; a few drops of yellow colour; 1 tsp of soap nut (reetha) water.

NOW:
1. Make a thin syrup of sugar and water and clean it with diluted milk.
2. Knead *paneer* till soft. Add flour and colour and knead till well-mixed and smooth.
3. Divide the mixture into 10 equal balls and shape into flat ovals.
4. Put strained syrup to boil. Place the *cham chams* carefully.

5. When it comes to boil again, add the *reetha* water in slow stream till all the *cham chams* are fully covered with froth.

6. Boil for 8 minutes. Now, cover half the vessel and boil for another five minutes.

7. Turn off fire. Let the *cham chams* soak in the syrup for four hours before serving.

8. Sprinkle rose water and serve.

Rasomalai

(ROSOGULLAS IN SWEET MILK)

Next to *rosogullas* this is the most popular Bengali sweet, outside Bengal.

You need

2 lt milk; 75 gm sugar; 20 *rosogullas;* ¼ lt extra milk; ¼ lt water.

NOW :

1. Boil 2 litres milk with the sugar and reduce to half. Reserve.
2. Mix water and the extra milk. Put to boil.
3. In the meanwhile, take out the *rosogullas* from the syrup. Squeeze well to drain as much of the syrup as you can.
4. When the milk and water mixture starts boiling, add 5–6 *rosogullas* at a time and boil for five minutes. Take out and keep aside.
5. Repeat and boil all the *rosogullas* this way.
6. Put the *rosogullas* in the thickened milk and simmer for a couple of minutes.
7. Cool refrigerate and serve.

Variation:

The milk may be flavoured with saffron and coloured yellow. Garnish with chopped nuts.

Mooger Borfi
(MOONG DAL FUDGE)

This was a favourite of Satyajit Ray. He had once mentioned this in an interview and also regretted the fact that *Mooger Borfi* was no longer available. An admirer of his had then sent him a box of this *burfi,* which pleased Ray no end.

You need

250 gm *moong dal;* 200 gm ghee; 200 gm sugar; 200 gm *khoya*; 200 ml water; 2 tbsp cashewnuts, broken; 2 tbsp raisins; 1 tsp rose water.

NOW:

1. Soak *moong dal* for five to six hours.
2. Drain and grind. But do not grind to a fine paste. It should be slightly granular like semolina.
3. Heat ghee in a *karahi*. Fry cashews and raisins. Keep aside.

4. Break *khoya* in tiny granules.
5. Make sugar syrup of 2-string consistency with sugar and water.
6. Fry *dal* paste in ghee over a slow fire till it starts leaving the sides of the *karahi*.
7. Add *khoya* and cook till everything gets mixed well.
8. Pour in the syrup and cook for a couple of minutes till it is of a fudge-like consistency.
9. Add rose water and pour on to a greased plate.
10. Decorate with cashewnuts and raisins.
11. When set, cut into squares or diamond-shaped pieces.

Balushahi
(INDIAN DOUGHNUTS)

You need good quality flour for *balushahi.* These will keep it for more than a week.

You need
500 gm flour; 100 gm ghee; 200 gm thick fresh curd; a pinch of baking soda; ½ tsp baking powder; 500 gm sugar; ghee for frying.

NOW:
1. Sieve the flour, baking powder and baking soda together. Cream the curd and 100 gm ghee together.
2. Knead the flour with this mixture. Do not knead vigorously. Use a light hand.

   Keep the dough aside for one hour.
3. Make a syrup with the sugar and 6 cups of water of 2-string consistency.

4. Now, knead the dough lightly once. Divide into lime-sized lumps. Roll each lump into round balls.
   Press lightly and make a slight indentation with a fingertip, in the middle.
   Make all the other *balushahis* thus.
5. Heat ghee in a *karahi* for deep frying.
6. Remove from fire when hot. Put in six *balushahis* at a time. Splash ghee on them with a spoon. Place pan again on low heat. The *balushahis* will bloat in size.
7. Fry to a light biscuit colour. Take out with a slotted spoon. Hold the spoon against the rim of the *karahi* so that any extra ghee can dip off.
8. Put the *balushahis* in the sugar syrup. Carefully stir them so that they are coated with the syrup.
9. When the *balushahis* have soaked in the syrup well, take out and keep aside to cool.
   When cold, the syrup will form a coating.

Makhane Ki Kheer
(LOTUS SEED KHEER)

Lotus seeds are widely eaten all over Northern India. Savoury dishes are made out of them as well. This *kheer*, easy to make, is particularly good.

You need

2½ lt milk; 50 gm lotus seeds; 50 gm raisins; 50 gm cashewnuts or almonds; 250 gm sugar.

NOW:

1. Clean and soak raisins. Blanch and finely slice the almonds, if using, or chop the cashews.
   Cut the lotus seeds in halves.
2. Put the milk to boil. When it comes to a boil, add the lotus seeds.
3. Cook until thick, like porridge.
4. Add sugar, nuts and raisins.
5. Cool and serve.

13

Kanchagolla

(SOFT SANDESH)

The curd used should be fresh and not sour. You may increase the amount of milk if you do not want to use condensed milk. Add 150 gm of sugar in that case.

You need

1 lt milk; ½ tin condensed milk; ½ cup curd; a little green cardamom powder.

NOW:

1. Bring milk to a boil. Cool and add curd.
2. Put on to boil. The mixture should curdle. If not, add a little lime juice.
3. As soon as the milk starts curdling, add the condensed milk. Stir continuously.
4. Stir well till the water evaporates and the mixture becomes a sticky mess.
5. Remove from fire and spread cardamom powder. Mix well.
6. When cool enough to handle, shape into balls.
7. This *sandesh* will not be smooth but granular in texture.

Kanchagolla

Notun Gurer Sandesh

Notun Gurer Sandesh
(DATE PALM JAGGERY SANDESH)

Like *notun gurer payesh,* you can make *notun gurer sandesh* also. *Gur* is added in a small quantity to impart a delicate beige colour and subtle flavour.

You need

½ **kg home made** *paneer;* **75 gm sugar; 50 gm jaggery.**
NOW:

1. The *paneer* must not have any water in it. Knead thoroughly until smooth and soft.
2. Make a syrup with the sugar and two tablespoons of water. Strain.
3. Add the *paneer* and grated jaggery into the syrup and put on heat.
4. Stir the whole mixture on a slow fire till the excess moisture dries up, but the mixture should be quite moist.
5. Let the mixture cool by stirring at intervals. This *sandesh* will not be very smooth.
6. When cold, divide into 15 portions. These can be shaped using moulds and decorated with raisins.

Gujiyas
(SWEET PUFFS)

These sweets are called *karanjis* in Maharashtra where the fillings are more varied, using *dals* and semolina.

You need

500 gm flour; 6 cup ghee; 500 gm *khoya*; 1 cup sugar; groundnut oil or ghee for frying.

NOW:

1. Mix the ghee with the flour until it resembles bread crumbs. Add water and knead to a soft dough.
2. Fry the khoya on low flame until the colour changes. Add sugar.
3. Divide the dough into lemon-sized balls.

    Roll out each ball like a *puri*.

Gujiya

Balushahi

4. Fill with *khoya*. Seal edges with a little water and twist the edges decoratively.

Puncture the *gujiyas* finely with a tooth pick, to prevent them from puffing up too much.

Deep fry in hot oil until golden.

Gajjar Ka Halwa
(CARROT HALWA)

This robust and filling dessert will be lapped up by even those who are not otherwise fond of carrots.

You need

1 kg carrots; 1 lt milk; 200 gm *khoya*; 200 gm sugar; 1 tsp green cardamom powder; 20 cashewnuts broken; 2 tbsp raisins; 4 tbsp ghee or groundnut oil.

NOW:

1. Wash, scrape and grate the carrots. Clean and soak the raisins for 20 minutes.

   Bread the *khoya* in granules.

2. Heat the ghee in a *karahi;* fry the raisins and take them out. Stir in the carrots. Cook, stirring them till they become darker in colour.

Gajjar Ka Halwa

Petha

3. Add the milk and cook till the milk evaporates and the mixture is thick. Keep stirring in between.
4. Halfway through, add the raisins and cashewnuts.
5. Put in the *khoya* and mix well. Stir well till the whole thing looks like a mass. Sprinkle green cardamom powder.
6. Tastes best when warm. Can be served cold, too.

Variation:

May use condensed milk instead of *khoya*.

In that case, omit sugar and reduce milk to 250 millilitre.

Pressure cook carrots in milk for three minutes and proceed with the recipe.

Petha
(ASH GOURD SWEET)

These *pethas* are sort of a preserve, particularly the dry ones that can be stored for days. They are also used in cakes and puddings. The syrupy ones are called *angoori petha.*Agra is famous for this kind of *pethas.*

You need good quality ripe ash gourd for making *petha.* The skin should be of whitish green colour.

You need

2 kg ash gourd; 20 gm lime (*chuna*—edible); 1 tsp alum powder; 1½ kg sugar; 1 tsp lime juice; 2 tbsp milk.

NOW:

1. Wash the ash gourd. Peel skin. Remove the pith and the seeds. Cut into pieces, 2.5 cm thick and 6 cm square.

2. Prick the pieces thoroughly with a stainless steel fork. Wash again.

3. Take one litre of water. Mix the lime. Soak the ash gourd pieces in it for four to five hours. Wash the pieces once again, thoroughly, so that all the lime is washed off.

4. Take another litre of water, add the alum powder and boil the ash gourd pieces in it for 20 minutes. Drain and wash once again so that no trace of lime and alum is left.

5. Mix the sugar with ½ litre water. Put to boil. Add 2 tablespoons milk mixed with 2 tablespoons water. Let the scum rise to the surface. Strain.

6. Boil the syrup again. Add 1 teaspoon lime juice and the ash gourd pieces. Boil till the syrup reaches 3-string consistency and the *petha* is done.

7. Any edible colour may be used in the syrup to colour the *pethas*.

Aamer Borfi

(MANGO FUDGE)

Take advantage of the mango season and make this delectable sweet.

You need

Fresh *paneer* made out of 1 lt of cow's milk; 1 cup mango pulp; 1 tsp green cardamom powder; 150 gm sugar; ¼ cup cashewnut pieces; a few drops of saffron colour.

NOW:

1. Knead *paneer* until smooth.
2. Put the mango pulp on medium fire in a *karahi*.
3. Stir constantly till thick.
4. Add sugar, green cardamom powder and the *paneer*.
5. Stir well until the mixture becomes quite thick and leaves the sides of the *karahi*.
6. Add saffron colour and cashew pieces.
7. Spread mixture in a greased square tray.
8. Cool and cut into pieces.

Halwa
(FLOUR PUDDING)

Halwas are typical North Indian sweet. These can be very simple—made with semolina and jaggery—or exotic with dry fruits and lots of ghee. Flour, wholemeal flour, gram flour, different kinds of *dals,* fruits and even eggs can be used.

You need
1 cup of wheat flour; ½ cup ghee; 3/4 cup jaggery or sugar; 1 cup milk; a handful of chestnuts, chopped; 1 tbsp raisins; ½ tsp nutmeg powder or cardamom powder or a mixture of both.

NOW:
1. Roast the flour in 2 tablespoons ghee till the colour changes and it gives out a fried aroma.

23

2. Dissolve the jaggery or sugar in milk. Add chopped cashewnuts and raisins.

3. Add the jaggery mixture to the flour and stir constantly. Continue to stir, otherwise it will turn into a lump. Keep on medium heat.

4. Also, keep on adding the ghee, one teaspoon at a time. When 1 teaspoon is absorbed, add another. By the time the ghee is finished, the mixture should be ready and thick. It should be golden brown in colour, and should leave the sides of the pan.

5. Add the nutmeg and cardamom powder. Excess ghee will float on top. Remove it, if you want to.

6. Serve hot.

Variation:

You may use semolina instead.

Imarti
(*DAL* FRITTERS IN SYRUP)

These are a kind of exotic *jalebi*. Made of a particular design, *imartis* are sold all over India, particularly North India.

You need
½ kg urad dal, without husk; 150 gm arrowroot; a few drops of orange colour; a few drops of saffron essence; 1½ kg sugar; ghee or groundnut oil for frying.

NOW:
1. Soak the *dal* overnight. Grind to a very smooth paste. Mix the colour and essence.
2. Now, add the arrowroot, a little at a time, till a batter of thick consistency is reached. If needed, add a little milk to get the correct consistency. It should be a little thicker than *pakoda* batter.
3. Make a syrup of 2-string consistency with sugar and 1½ cups of water.
4. Take a piece of thick cloth. Make a hole in the centre. Gather the

ends to make a bag. Put as much batter in it as it can hold comfortably. You may also use a plastic bottle with a hole in the cap, or even a meringue bag with a small nozzle.

5. Heat the ghee or groundnut oil in a *karahi*.
6. Press the cloth to make a circle of the batter. Now, quickly move the bag in a circular motion to make tiny rings on the chain. This is the typical *imarti* pattern.
7. Likewise, make other *imartis. Make* as many as the *karahi* will hold comfortably at a time.
8. Fry on medium heat. When of a golden colour, take out with the help of a stick. Lay the stick against the *karahi* so that extra ghee may drip off.
9. Soak in the syrup for 15 minutes.
10. Take out and keep one above the other. Decorate with silver foil, if you want.

Variation:

May use *moong dal* batter. In that case, add half a cup of curd to it. You may leave out arrowroot. Rest of the process is the same.

Imarti

Motichoor Laddoo

Pinni

(RICE FLOUR FUDGE)

You need

250 gm rice flour; 175 gm sugar or *boora*—powdered *desi* sugar; 100 gm ghee; 25 gm raisins; 25 gm mixed nuts, chopped.

NOW:

1. Roast the rice flour in ghee. Do not let it colour.
2. Remove from heat when it starts emitting a fried aroma.
3. Mix in the powdered sugar, raisins and chopped nuts.
4. When cool enough to handle, take a fistful and press. You will find ridges patterned on the *pinni*. These keep well.

Variation:

Instead of rice flour, use 100 gm wheat flour and 100 gm *khoya*.

Fry wheat flour until golden. Add *khoya* and cook for a few minutes on low heat.

Proceed with the rest of the recipe.

Motichoor Laddoo
(FRIED GRAM FLOUR BALL)

No festival in India, particularly in the northern and central parts, is complete without *motichoor laddoos*. These are traditionally made during marriages and sent to friends and relations.

You need

½ kg gram flour; ½ kg sugar; a pinch of baking powder; ¼ cup milk; a few drops of orange colour; a few drops of saffron essence; 2 tsp cardamom powder; 2 tbsp finely chopped blanced almonds; ghee for frying.

NOW:

1. Sieve gram flour and baking powder together. Mix in 2 tablespoons melted ghee, milk and enough water to make a thickish batter, say, like *pakoda* batter.

2. Heat enough ghee in a *karahi*. Take a perforated spoon with tiny holes in it.

3. When the ghee is smoking hot, hold the perforated spoon in one hand and rub some of the batter with the other so that the batter falls in tiny droplets. Tap the handle of the perforated spoon against the rim of the *karahi* to make the mixture fall through.

   Fry till golden. Take the *boondis* out with another perforated ladle, resting it on the rim of the pan for a while, so that the extra ghee drips down to the *karahi*. Likewise, fry all the *boondis*.

5. In the meanwhile, prepare a syrup of 3-string consistency. Add colour and essence. Keep the syrup hot.

6. Put in the fried *boondis* directly in the syrup, also add the almonds and cardamom powder. Mix thoroughly.

7. When tolerably cold, form into round balls with greased palms.

8. These will be quite soft *laddoos*. If you want hard ones, cook the syrup till hard ball stage (a drop of syrup put into cold water forms a hard ball).

Jalebi
(SYRUPY SPIRALS)

These syrupy delights are popular all over India. Throughout Northern India, hot *jalebis* and hot milk are consumed at breakfast.

You need

120 gm flour; 55 gm corn flour or gram flour; 30 gm curd; 2 tbsp hot oil; a few drops of saffron colour; 225 gm sugar; 100 ml water; ½ tsp lime juice; 375 ml ghee or groundnut oil.

NOW:

1. Sift flour and corn flour or gram flour together.
2. Beat curd and add to the flour mixture. Mix thoroughly.
3. Pour the hot oil into the mixture and blend well. Add enough warm water to make a smooth batter of pouring consistency.

Jalebi

Besan Laddoo

4. Set aside for 24 hours to ferment. Add colour to the fermented batter.
5. Mix sugar with water and make a syrup of 1-string consistency. Add lime juice and strain. Keep it warm.
6. Make a hole in the centre of a thick piece of cloth from which the batter can pass through. A meringue bag may also be used for this purpose.
7. Heat ghee or oil in a *karahi*. Press the batter directly into the hot ghee in spirals.
8. Fry at low heat till crisp and golden.
9. Drain and immediately immerse in the warm syrup for about a minute. Then remove with a skewer resting against the rim for a few seconds.

Serve hot or cold.

Variation:

A jaggery syrup may be used instead. Boil 250 gm jaggery into 3/4 cup of water and make a syrup of 1-string consistency.

Besan Laddoo
(GRAM FLOUR BALL)

I adore these *besan laddoos*. I always bring a boxful whenever I visit my mother in Delhi.

You need

500 gm gram flour; 500 gm powdered sugar; 200 gm ghee; 1 tsp cardamom powder.

NOW:

1. Sift the gram flour. No lumps should remain.
2. Heat the ghee until smoking hot. Lower the heat. Put in the gram flour and fry on medium heat until golden. It will also give out a lovely fried aroma.
3. Take off fire. Wait for two minutes and add the powdered sugar.
4. Cool till bearably hot and form into round balls with greased palms.
5. Set aside to harden. Store in an airtight container. They keep well for quite sometime.

Pedha
(SOLIDIFIED MILK FUDGE)

The city of Mathura in U.P. is well-known for *pedhas*. So is the city of Benaras. There are a number of variations.

You need

½ kg *khoya*; 250 gm *khadi shakkar* powder or *shakkar ka bura,* which is a *desi* variety of sugar available in the market. Powdered sugar may be substituted; 250 ml milk; 2 drops of rose essence; 2 tbsp of finely chopped almonds and pistachios; 1 tsp green cardamom powder.

NOW:

1. Mix *khoya* and *shakkar* together and put on medium heat.
2. Add 2 tbsp of milk and stir. When the milk gets absorbed, add another 2 tbsp of milk. Stir with the back of a heavy ladle as this will smoothen

out the lumps. This way add all the milk. If need be, lower heat further. When all the milk gets absorbed and the *khoya* is still quite moist, remove from heat.

3. Mix the rose essence with a little sugar and mix with the *khoya* well.

4. In another plate, mix the finely chopped nuts and the cardamom powder.

5. Take a small lump of the *khoya* mixture, press on the nuts and remove. Likewise, make all the pedas.

Variation:

Add saffron dissolved in a little milk instead of rose essence to make *kesari pedhas*.

Steamed Modak

You need

For the casing: ½ kg rice powder; a pinch of salt; 1 tsp groundnut oil; for the filling: 2 coconuts grated; 1 kg jaggery or sugar; 25 raisins; 1 tsp green cardamom powder.

NOW:

For the Casing :

1. In a thick-bottomed pan, heat water 1½ times the volume of the rice powder. When the water starts boiling, add the salt and the oil. Add the rice powder all at once.

2. Stir well till no lumps remain. Lower flame. Cover and cook for seven minutes or until the rice flour forms into a lump. Remove.

3. When the rice is cool enough to handle, knead it into a soft smooth dough with greased palms.

35

For the filling:

1. Place a *karahi* with half tablespoon of ghee on fire. Put in the grated coconut and fry while on medium fire. Add sugar or jaggery and raisins.

   Cook on medium fire, stirring occasionally till the mixture is almost dry. This will take at least 15 minutes. Keep aside.

2. Now, take a lime-sized ball from the ready dough and shape into a smooth ball.

   Make a hollow in the middle and put a little coconut mixture in it, pressing it down gently. Pull up the sides carefully, pinching them at the top, giving it a conical shape.

   Make all the *modaks* the same way.

3. Steam them in a colander over boiling water. Place a muslin cloth or a banana leaf over the colander. Place as many *modaks* as it comfortably holds. Steam for eight to ten minutes.

   A pressure cooker may also be used.

Shrikhand
(YOGURT WITH SUGAR AND NUTS)

This is certainly one of the choicest of the Indian desserts. It is satin smooth and a treat for every age.

You need

3 lt milk; 1 tbsp curd; sugar equal in quantity to curd; 5 green cardamoms, powdered; ½ tsp nutmeg powder; a few strands of saffron; a few chopped cashewnuts and almonds.

NOW:

1. Boil the milk and let cool. When tepid, add the curd and mix well. Cover well and keep in a warm place to set overnight.

2. Next morning, pour the curd into a white muslin cloth and tie the edges into a firm knot. Let it hang till all the whey is completely drained out. This will at least take four to five hours.

3. Remove the thick curd from the cloth and mix well with the sugar. Strain the mixture through a thin cloth or a strainer.

4. Lightly roast the saffron strands on a *tawa* and powder them.

5. Add saffron, cardamom and nutmeg to the Shrikhand and mix well, using a mixer, if necessary, for a smooth consistency.

6. Garnish with chopped nuts.

7. Serve chilled.

Variation:

Shrikhand can be made without saffron or nuts. Fresh fruits can be mixed instead, before serving.

Mava Malido
(EGG AND SEMOLINA PUDDING)

A Parsi delicacy.

You need

50 gm of flour; 50 gm whole wheat flour; 50 gm semolina; 100 gm *khoya*; ¼ cup milk; 250 gm sugar; ½ cup of water; 2 eggs; 1 tsp vanilla essence; 6 green cardamoms; ½ tsp nutmeg; 15 almonds; 15 cashewnuts; 15 raisins; 2 tbsp chopped glace cherries; 2 tbsp chopped orange peel; 150 gm pure ghee.

NOW :

1. Blanch and slice almonds. Chop cashewnuts, clean raisins. Fry all these in 1 tablespoon ghee and set aside after draining.

2. Sift together flour, semolina and whole wheat flour (*atta*).

3. Powder the green cardamoms and nutmeg.

39

4. Mix the sifted ingredients with 100 gm ghee and the milk and keep aside for half an hour.

5. Cook on a slow fire, stirring constantly with a wooden spoon until the mixture thickens and becomes light brown in colour. Cool. Mix with the *khoya* and keep aside.

6. Make a thickish syrup with the sugar and water. Add to the *khoya* mixture along with left-over ghee, and keep stirring with a spoon over a very slow fire.

7. When it thickens a little, take off fire. Slowly pour the egg into the *khoya* mixture. Beat thoroughly.

8. Cook again on a slow flame stirring until the ghee floats on top.

9. Remove from fire and add vanilla, cardamom, nutmeg, half the fried dry fruits, half the cherries and peel. Mix together.

10 Decorate with the rest.

11. Can be kept well under refrigeration for a month. But serve either lukewarm or at room temperature.

Koomas
(PARSI CAKE)

You need

½ cup flour; 1½ cups semolina; 6 eggs; ½ cup milk; 1 tsp vanilla; 1 cup sugar; ½ tsp cardamom powder; ½ tsp nutmeg powder; 2 tbsp blanched and slice almonds; 1 tsp dried yeast or 2 tsp fresh yeast; 180 gm ghee or butter.

NOW:

1. Mix the yeast with 1 tablespoon lukewarm water, 1 teaspoon sugar and 1 teaspoon flour and keep in a warm place for fifteen minutes.

2. Cream the butter or ghee and sugar until soft. Add eggs one by one, beating well after each addition.

3. Mix the yeast mixture now. It should be quite frothy, by now.

4. Add the sieved flour and semolina and the milk lightly. Mix in the

essence, spices and almonds.

5. Cover well and leave in a warm place to rise.
6. When double in bulk, mix once to release the gas and place in a greased baking pan.
7. Bake in a moderate oven till done.

Baath
(GOAN CAKE)

This simple cake from Goa is quite easy to prepare. The use of semolina marks a refreshing change.

You need

½ kg semolina; 6 eggs; 8 tbsp butter or ghee; 2 coconuts; rose water as needed; 200 gm sugar; 1 tbsp caraway seeds; ½ tsp salt; ½ tsp salt; ½ tsp baking powder.

NOW:

1. Separate the whites and the yolks of the eggs.
2. Beat the butter or ghee and the sugar until light and fluffy. Beat in the egg yolks one by one until well-mixed.
3. Roast the caraway seeds without any ghee until golden. Keep aside.

4. Grate the coconut. See to it that no brown part is grated. Grind with the rose water to a fine paste.

5. Add semolina to the prepared butter and egg batter. Mix well. Blend in the baking powder and the caraway seeds.

6. Beat the egg whites till fluffy and add to the mixture lightly.

7. Pour in two greased and floured baking tins.

8. Bake in a moderate oven until done.

Mohanthaal
(MAHARASHTRIAN GRAM FLOUR FUDGE)

This fudge from Maharashtra differs in taste and texture from the popular *Mysore pak* of South India.

You need

½ kg gram flour; ¼ kg ghee; ¼ lt milk; ¾ kg sugar; 100 gm *khoya;*
½ cup chopped nuts and raisins; 1 tsp cardamom powder;
½ tsp nutmeg powder.

NOW:

1. Heat the milk and 1 tablespoon of ghee together.
2. Rub in half the ghee to the gram flour. Add half the milk. Mix well and keep aside for half an hour. Pass mixture through a sieve so that no lumps remain.

3. Heat the remaining ghee in a *karahi*. Fry the gram flour on low heat till light brown; a lovely aroma emanates.

4. Add the grated *khoya*. Fry for some more time until the mixture becomes a shade more golden.

5. Put in the rest of the milk. Stir until the milk is absorbed. Mix in the cardamom and nutmeg powder.

6. In another pan, put the sugar with half a cup of water. Boil until the soft ball stage. Remove from heat.

7. Pour the gram flour mixture and the nuts and the raisins into the syrup. Mix well. The syrup should be totally absorbed by the flour mixture.

8. Spread in a greased tray. Level the surface with the back of a *katori*. Cut into squares when set.

Puran Poli
(STUFFED SWEET PANCAKES)

This traditional Maharashtrian sweet is served on almost all festive occasions.

You need
For the pancakes : 1 cup flour; 1 cup wholemeal flour (atta); 75 gm ghee; For the stuffing: ¾ cup gram *dal*; ¾ cup jaggery or sugar; 1 tsp green cardamom powder; ½ tsp nutmeg powder; 2 tbsp groundnut oil; ghee for frying.

NOW:
1. Pressure cook the *dal* with two cups of water for ten minutes. When cool, strain.
2. Heat the oil in a *karahi*. Put in the boiled *dal,* sugar or jaggery. Stir and cook till dry.

3. Cool and grind with the cardamom and nutmeg powder.
4. Mix the flour and the *atta* together. Rub in 75 gm of the ghee. With the help of a little milk, make a soft dough.
5. Divide the dough into small balls and make thin *poli*.
6. Place a little filling on one half of the *poli* leaving a slight space around the sides. Cover with the other half of the circle. Press the side and crimp so that the *poli* gets stuck.
7. Shallow fry on a *tawa* until light golden.
8. Serve with hot milk or ghee.

Puran Poli

Khajuri Ghari

Khajur Ghari
(PASTRY ENCRUSTED DATES)

From Parsi cuisine. Serve hot at tea time.

You need

For the pastry : 2 cups flour; 1 tsp baking powder; a pinch of salt; 1 tbsp ghee; For the date mixture: 250 gm dates, seeded; ½ tbsp sugar; ½ tbsp ghee; 2½ tbsp sugar; ½ tsp cardamom and nutmeg, each powdered.

NOW:

For the Pastry:
1. Sift flour, baking powder, and salt together. Add ghee and knead well with a little rose water until soft and smooth.
2. Roll out in a large circle, spread with 1 tbsp ghee and 1 tbsp flour.
3. Roll up like a Swiss roll—that is, start rolling from the end nearest to you, but roll away from you. Roll tightly, as you would roll a mat.

4. Cut into small portions. Roll each portion into a ball.
5. Roll up each ball into small rounds. Spread with dates mixture and top with another round. Seal edges.
6. Shallow fry till golden brown and cooked.

For the Date Mixture :

1. Mince dates in a mixer.
2. Heat ghee and add sugar. When sugar melts, add dates. Cool till the dates are fried and sticky and the mixture soft.
3. Add the spice powders. Blend well and let cool.

Lagan Nu Kastar
(BAKED WEDDING CUSTARD)

No Parsi wedding is complete without this custard.

You need

2½ lt milk; 500 gm sugar; 6 eggs; 1 tsp nutmeg powder; 1 tsp vanilla essence; 50 gm chopped cashewnuts.

NOW:

1. Beat the eggs.
2. Boil the milk. Keep stirring continuously. Add sugar.
3. Boil until the milk is reduced to half its original volume.
4. Add powdered nutmeg and keep aside to cool.
5. When thoroughly cooled, add the well-beaten eggs, nuts and vanilla.
6. Blend well and pour into a greased baking dish.
7. Bake in a moderate oven till golden brown, and the custard is firm.
8. Cut in wedges and serve.

Dahitran

(YOGURT ROUNDS IN SYRUP)

You need

1 cup flour; 1 cup semolina; 1 cup yogurt; 1 cup sugar; 1 tbsp ghee; 1 tbsp rose water; a pinch of baking powder; ½ tsp cardamom powder; ½ tsp nutmeg powder; ghee or groundnut oil for deep frying.

NOW:

1. Sift flour, semolina, baking powder, cardamom and nutmeg powder together.
2. Hand the yogurt in a muslin cloth to let whey drain.
3. Rub in the ghee with the flour mixture.
4. Now add yogurt and knead well to assort smooth dough—add a little warm water, if needed.
5. Cover well and let stand for at least three hours so that it can rise.
6. Make a syrup of 1-string consistency with the sugar and ¼ cup of water. Add rose water when cool.

7. Heat oil in a *karahi*.
8. Break small lumps of the dough and flatten into small rounds with your palm. Grease your palm so that the dough does not stick.
9. Deep fry until golden brown.
10. Soak the *dahitrans* in the syrup or they may just be dropped in the syrup and taken out immediately.

Mysore Pak
(GRAM FLOUR FUDGE)

This lovely fudge from South India has a ganular texture. Do not be alarmed by the excessive amount of ghee used. Most of it can be drained out at the end of the cooking process.

You need
250 gm gram flour; 250 gm sugar; 400 gm ghee.

NOW:

1. Roast the gram flour in 4 tablespoons ghee until golden and fragrant.
2. Make a thin sugar syrup with the sugar and a cup of water.
3. Now, on low heat keep stirring the syrup with one hand and pour the roasted gram flour a little at a time, with the other hand. Mix the syrup and flour well, ensuring that there are no lumps and the mixture is smooth.

Mysore Pak

Pongal

4. In a separate pan boil the ghee.

5. Gradually, add 3–4 tablespoons ghee at a time to the flour and sugar mixture, while it is still on fire. Keep on stirring constantly on a medium flame.

6. When all the ghee is added and the mixture is reddish brown and bubbly with ghee oozing out from the sides, pour it into a deep, large and flat tray. Spread it evenly. Keep the tray tilted so that any extra ghee can drain out. Remove this drained out ghee.

7. Cut into squares when slightly cold.

Sevian Ka Muzaffar
(VERMICELLI SWEET–III)

All these vermicelli sweets are made in the Hyderabadi tradition.

You need

250 gm fine vermicelli; 500 gm sugar; 1 lt milk; 100 gm ghee; 50 gm dessicated coconut; 8 green cardamoms; 10–12 drops of *kewra* water.

NOW:

1. Break the vermicelli in small pieces and dry roast them until pink. Set aside.
2. Heat ghee in a *degchi* and put in the pounded cardamoms. When they puff up, add sugar and milk.
3. When milk reduces to half its volume, add vermicelli and dessicated coconut.
4. Cook till done.
5. Sprinkle with *kewra* water and serve hot or cold as desired.

Pal Payasam
(KHEER WITH RICE FLOUR DUMPLINGS)

A favourite with the Tamilians. This is also offered to Lord Krishna. Can be served warm or cold.

You need

For the *polis;* 200 gm flour; 3 tbsp groundnut oil; For the *kheer;* 1 lt milk; 125 gm sugar; 1 tsp green cardamom powder; ½ tsp nutmeg powder.

NOW:

For the *Polis*:

1. Rub oil into the flour well. Knead with water to make a soft dough. Divide into 15 balls.

2. Roll each into a small *poli*. Deep fry one at a time.

57

For the *Kheer:*

1. Boil the milk till it is reduced to half its original volume. Add sugar and boil further till one-third remains. Add cardamom and nutmeg powder. Remove.

2. When lukewarm, dip the *polis* and serve warm or cold.

Paruppu Payasam
(MOONG DAL KHEER)

This is very popular in Kerala. It is a must for *Onam*, the harvest festival, and *Vishu*—the new year.

You need

1 cup *moong dal*; 3 cups water; 1 cup coconut milk; 1 cup sugar or jaggery; ¼ tsp cardamom powder; 1 cup milk.

NOW:

1. Roast *dal* in a pan till brown flakes appear and a fried aroma emanates.
2. Bring water to a boil in a saucepan. Add the *dal* and boil until it is very soft.
3. Add the coconut milk and sugar to the boiled *dal*.
4. Boil for ten minutes. Add the milk. Stir occasionally.
5. Remove from heat and add cardamom powder. Stir.
6. Cool and serve.

Pongal
(RICE AND DAL SWEET)

The most important festival in Tamil Nadu is *Pongal*—the harvest festival, celebrated at the beginning of the Tamil month of *Thai*.

Pongal, which literally means boiled rice, is an occasion for great rejoicing in the villages and elsewhere. Various types of *pongal* is cooked, including this sweet pongal called *sarkarai pongal* in Tamil and *Chakkera Pongal* in Telugu.

You need
2 cups basmati rice; 1 cup *moong dal*; 1 cup bengal gram *dal;* ½ coconut grated; 2 cups jaggery; 10 small cardamoms; 5 tsp pure ghee; 2 cups milk; 10 chopped cashwenuts; 10 raisins.

NOW:
1. Roast both the *dals* in a *karahi* till light brown.

2. Wash rice. Boil rice, *dals* and two cups of milk and two cups of water in a pressure cooker for five minutes.

3. Boil the jaggery with ¼ cup of water till the jaggery melts. Strain.

4. Add this jaggery syrup and 3 teaspoons ghee to the rice mixture and put on a low heat for five minutes. Stir in between.

5. Heat the remaining ghee in a *karahi*. Fry the nuts and raisins and the grated coconut till pink.

6. Mix with the rice mixture.

7. Decorate with the cardamom powder.

Double Ka Mitha
(BREAD SWEET)

An exotic pudding of the Mughal days, this delicacy continues to enjoy popularity even today.

You Need

1½ lt milk; 8 slices bread; 150 gm ghee; 350 gm sugar; 1 cup water; 20 raisins; ½ tsp nutmeg powder; ½ tsp cardamom powder; a pinch of saffron; a few drops of orange colour; 250 gm *khoya*.

NOW:

1. Halve the bread slices after removing the crusts. Roast and crush the saffron.

2. Boil milk till reduced to half. Add *khoya* and cook together till thick, like cream. Mix saffron, nutmeg and cardamom powder.

3. Fry the bread slices in ghee until golden. Soak the fried bread in the thickened milk for 15 minutes.
4. Make a thickish sugar syrup and pour over the bread. Sprinkle the raisins on top.
5. Transfer the whole thing in a greased oven-proof dish.
6. Bake in a moderate oven till golden.

Adirasam
(SWEET RICE)

You Need

1 cup rice; 1 cup jaggery; ½ tbsp poppy seeds; 4 small cardamoms, powdered; oil for deep frying.

NOW:

1. Clean and soak rice in water for an hour.
2. Drain and pound to a fine powder.
3. Roast poppy seeds and sesame seeds. Add to rice powder. Spread on a newspaper for ten minutes.
4. Make a jaggery syrup of thick consistency.
5. Put on medium flame. Add rice flour and go on stirring. Add powdered cardamoms.

6. Remove from fire and let cool.
7. Make small lime-sized balls. Pat in your palm with a little oil.
8. Heat groundnut oil in a *karahi*. Deep fry the balls till crisp and brown.
9. Drain and store in an airtight tin.

Sweet Murukku

In South Indian households *murukkus* are made in both sweet and savoury forms. These are especially made and stored for guests.

You Need

5 cups rice; 1 cup *urad dal*; 1 kg jaggery; 5 cardamoms; 5 peppercorns; groundnut oil for frying.

NOW:

1. Coarsely powder both the cardamoms and the peppercorns.
2. Powder both the *dal* and rice.
3. Mix with water and form a stiff dough.
4. Put in a *murukku* mould and press.
5. Deep fry in oil. Make all the *murukkus* thus.

6. Boil jaggery with a little water and make a thick syrup. Add the coarsely powdered spices.

7. Break all the *murukkus* in 2.5 cm pieces and mix with the jaggery syrup.

8. Grease your palms and roll the mixture into small balls. Leave to cool.

Gil-e-firdaus

A Hyderabadi delicacy. Amply demonstrates how even the humble gourd can be turned into an exotic sweet.

You Need

1 kg bottle gourd; 1 lt milk; 700 gm *khoya;* 15 almonds; a few strands of saffron; 75 gm sugar; 1 tsp cardamom powder; 1 pinch of alum powder; ½ tsp *kewra* water (vetivier).

NOW:

1. Blanch and finely slice the almonds. Soak saffron in 1 tablespoon milk.

2. Peel the bottle gourd. Discard pith and seeds. Coarsely grate the gourd.

3. Boil 2 cups of water with the alum powder in a *degchi*. Put a stainless steel sieve on it and keep the gourd in it. Cover and steam till soft.

4. Now, loosely tie the gourd in a thin piece of cloth and hang for two hours till the extra water is drained.

5. Boil the milk with the sugar till reduced to half its original volume. Mix the *khoya* in it.

6. When the *khoya* has totally mixed with the milk, add the gourd and cook for five minutes. The gourd should be cooked but must not totally dissolve.

7. Remove from fire and add *kewra* water and the saffron. When cold, decorate with almonds and serve.

Sapno Ka Meethas
(VERMICELLI SWEET-II)

I really like these high flown, romantic names given to the vermicelli during the Mughal age. The names have carried till this day. The recipes have been simplified somewhat. We use less ghee (often substituted with groundnut oil) and nuts now.

You Need

250 gm thick vermicelli; 2 lt milk; 300 gm sugar; 100 gm *makhana* (lotus seeds); 10 almonds.

NOW:

1. Blanch and slice almonds.
2. In a large pan, roast the vermicelli slightly. Set aside.

3. Put together the milk, sugar, vermicelli and *makhana* on low-medium heat and cook until milk is reduced to half its original volume. Keep stirring throughout.

4. When the vermicelli gets cooked and well-mixed with the *kheer*, add almonds and cook for another three minutes.

5. You may decorate with additional dry fruits.

6. Serve hot or at room temperature.

Aam Kalakanda
(MANGO FUDGE)

You need

1 lt full cream milk; 125 gm sugar; 1 cup mango pulp, preferably the *daseri* variety; 4 pinches of tartaric acid; 5 drops of orange colour; ½ tsp green cardamom powder; 1 tbsp chopped nuts; 1 silver foil.

NOW:

1. Put the sugar to boil, on high heat.

2. Add a pinch of tartaric acid. Keep stirring.

3. After about a couple of minutes, add another pinch of tartaric acid. Stir likewise; add all the acid, one pinch at a time. Let the milk boil and keep stirring. This will make the milk granular without actually curdling it.

4. When the milk becomes thick, add sugar and mango pulp and let cool.
5. Reduce heat. When the mixture thickens further and bubbles form on the surface, add the colour. Mix well.
6. Pour into a greased tray.
7. Cut into desired shapes. When cold, decorate with silver foil.

Ramras Chawal
(MANGO PULP WITH RICE)

You need

250 gm very good quality basmati rice; 2 cups mango pulp, preferably the *daseri* variety; a small pinch of saffron, soaked in 1 tbsp milk; 4 cloves; a few drops of edible orange colour; 3 tbsp pure ghee; 2 tbsp chopped nuts; silver foil for decoration.

NOW:

1. Pick, wash and drain rice.

2. Heat 2 tablespoons ghee in a heavy-bottomed *degchi*.

3. Season with the cloves.

4. Add rice. Fry for two minutes.

5. Add 300 ml hot water. Cover and cook on low heat.

6. When the water dries up, add the mango pulp and sugar.

7. Let it cook on low heat. Remove when done and sprinkle a tablespoon of ghee.

8. Decorate with chopped nuts and silver foil. May be served hot or cold.